My First Biography

Harriet Tubman

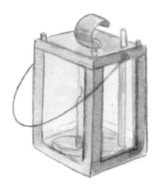

by Marion Dane Bauer
Illustrated by Tammie Lyon

SCHOLASTIC INC.
New York   Toronto   London   Auckland
Sydney   Mexico City   New Delhi   Hong Kong

ISBN 978-0-545-23257-9

Text copyright © 2010 by Marion Dane Bauer
Illustrations copyright © 2010 by Tammie Lyon

12 11 10 9 8 7 6 5 4   12 13 14 15/0
Printed in the U.S.A.   40
First printing, September 2010

Book design by Jennifer Rinaldi Windau

Harriet Tubman was born in the United States of America.
She was born a slave.

Her parents were slaves.

Her brothers and sisters were slaves.

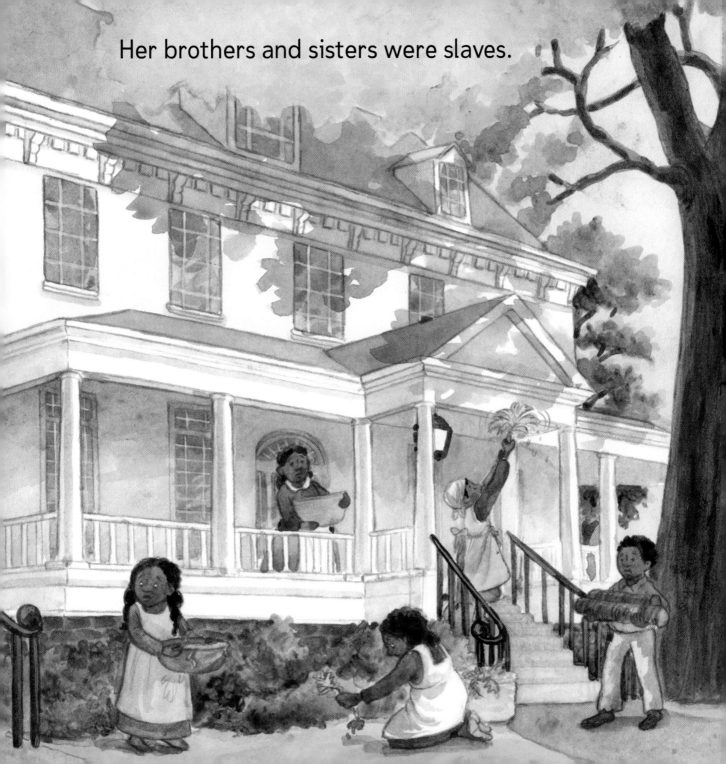

To be a slave meant that someone else owned you.

That person could make you work very, very hard.

That person could even sell you like a sack of potatoes.

Harriet didn't want to be a slave.
She wanted to be free.

When Harriet was grown, she ran away from the South where she had always lived.

She traveled at night, following the North Star.
She trudged through woods and swamps.

Some good people helped her reach the North
where no one was allowed to own slaves.

At last, she was free!

But her parents and her brothers
and her sisters were still slaves.

So Harriet made the dangerous journey to the South again.

She brought her sister and her sister's
two children back north with her.

She traveled south many times,
always hiding, always moving at night.

She brought hundreds of slaves to freedom.

She brought her brothers and her parents, too.

Then in 1861, the North went to war with the South.

Harriet became a nurse, a cook, and a spy.
She even led troops to rescue more slaves.

When the Civil War ended and the slaves were freed,
Harriet worked for rights for women . . . all women.

She also set up a home for old and poor black people.

She brought her parents to live there.

PENNSYLVANIA

Philadelphia

Kennett Square

Wilmington

NEW

Odessa

Blackbird

Harriet Tubman

Black Heritage USA 13¢

Dover

Camden

Hazlettville

Willow Grove

Sandtown

KENT

DELAW

Greensboro

Baltimore

Danton

MARYLAND

TALBOT

Easton

CAROLINE

Preston

Federalsburg

Poplar
Neck

Bellevue

CHESAPEAKE BAY

Madison

Cambridge

Church Creek

DORCHESTER

Bucktown

GREAT SALE
of
SLAVES

JANUARY 10, 1855

3 MALES Aged from 29 to 28, Strong
1 FEMALE Aged 42, Bigner
1 FEMALE Aged 52
1 MALE Aged

Harriet Tubman was born a slave, but she didn't stay a slave.
She became a proud, strong, free woman.

THREE HUNDRED DOLLARS REWARD.

R ANAWAY from the subscriber on Mo
the 17th ult., three negroes, named
lows: HARRY, aged about 19 ye
on one side of his neck a wen, ji
the ear, he is of a dark chestnut col
et 8 or 9 inches hight; BEN, aged
25 years, is very quick to speak w
o, he is of a chestnut color, about
MINTY, aged about 27 years, is o
stnut color, fine looking, and about 5
gh. One hundred dollars reward
given for each of the above named ne-
taken out of the State, and $50 each if
n the State. They must be lodged in
e, Easton or Cambridge Jail, in Mary-
ELIZA

Harriet Tubman is an American hero!